Night Madre

poems by

Kay Reid

Finishing Line Press
Georgetown, Kentucky

Night Madre

Copyright © 2024 by Kay Reid
ISBN 979-8-88838-771-9 First Edition
All rights reserved under International and Pan-American Copyright Conventions.
No part of this book may be reproduced in any manner whatsoever without written permission from the publisher, except in the case of brief quotations embodied in critical articles and reviews.

ACKNOWLEDGMENTS

I thank Michael Ward,
Editor and colleague, for his invaluable contribution to this book,
and Sharon Chalem, photographer and colleague, for hers.
I also thank Joan Maiers for her insights.

Publisher: Leah Huete de Maines
Editor: Christen Kincaid
Cover Design: Elizabeth Maines McCleavy
Author Photo: Sharon Chalem

Order online: www.finishinglinepress.com
　　　　　also available on amazon.com

Author inquiries and mail orders:
Finishing Line Press
PO Box 1626
Georgetown, Kentucky 40324
USA

Contents

Section I Word, Birth Memory

Tattoos 1
Remember, Joseph 3
To Remember Exactly 4
I Am It, the Thick 5
Rockaway 6
Why I Like Bad Poetry 8

Section II Hagar and Astyanax

Hagar the Brave 13
The Return of Hagar 14
Night Madre, Be 15
Beware the Laurel 16
Night Madre Beholden 17
Darling Night Madre 18
Night Madre Forlorn 19
Astyanax Did not Die 20
Astyanax, at Rest 21
Astyanax, Please 22

Section III, Enigma, Neighbor

A Rusty Beard 25
My Neighbor 26
Enigma 27
A Kettle 28
Madison Street 29
Little Jasmine 30
True Selves 31
What Must One Do to Be Saved 32
Ballot Box 34

Section I

Word, Birth, Memory

Tattoos

As I grow ancient,
let tattoos appear
all over my body.
I will consult them
for evidence of what I've been.

A rococo ring on the wedding finger,
dreams needled in,
the burning.
On my soft stomach
one small image allowed,
an infant in a cap with bells.
I will rest my tired hand on him,
staring at Tuscan hills.

On my upper left arm,
the tiny replica
of a revolutionary joke book
I wrote,
its pages resembling an ancient hymnal.
On the right,
an erotic pose,
myself and the one I love.
Perhaps my old brown shawl
will conceal us.

And on my calves and thighs,
trellises of roses and climbing ivy
over the veins and their rivers of years.
I shall be a work of ambulatory art
on the beaches of Greece,
rolling my jeans up high.

My body shall greatly entertain
doctors and nurses,
on that dreaded day,
when my last love is a touch
only I will remember.

They may not enhance my face at all.
Let granddaughter know its plain, strained self
as she watches the pine box fall.

Remember, Joseph

It was a cave,
when the story entered,
brushing my legs.
All the stars were pleased,
earth was aroused.

In the fields
in the mountains,
crystals in every crevasse.
Snow, green and silver,
sprinkled rock, dune and tree.
Earth stung with its sheen.

And an angel
descended and spoke
to workers in the dirt,
          "Get up, get up,
             a story has bitten the earth!"

Rich men,
Diplomats with fat hands
acquainted with incense,
good luck and seven course dinners
sensed the challenge
on earth,

and searching for us
found the cave
where our story
breathed warmly in its
thousands of pores,

and you, standing there in the straw
in your ragged green coat
denied you ever knew me.

To Remember Exactly

your warmth on my left hip,
arms around your plumpness,
fingers webbed out
on your torso buttoned
in yellow corduroy.
Simply to remember
the mass of your body
wiggling on my bones
and becoming quiet,
like words settling finally
on an unfinished letter.
Then, the hand, the right hand,
stirring oats into the bowl,
moving the bowl
to our place,
moving us to the squat burgundy chair,
placing you on
my upper left femur,
your entire self
leaning against my pelvic girdle.
You, receiving small runny bites,
sticky corduroy suit
on my long sweater.
Tasting
these twenty-eight years.

I Am It, the Thick

mattress of skin
buttons to pick
teeth everywhere
smiling the little soul to sleep

I offer him a cup of milk
in a sparkling thimble
balanced upon my little finger
sitting on the window sill

I am the jester
with hands
that render scoop
pick up put down
two monster flicks
swooshing shadows
holding withholding

the huge one
who covers the door
vanishing
appearing
like spider squash
2000 arms
a Medusa transforming
fists to stars
figs to jam,
an enlarged jar of raisins
spilling

I am enormous,
the choir at 6 a.m.
oh Jesus Christ at dusk
I am the huge one
who comes and goes

Rockaway

Will you forgive, oh please
Will you—
That I didn't have—
—compare it to when coyote grabbed our bunny—
I didn't have
Money that anxious Rockaway
At the cabin

Promising them, the jeans, next month
Stepping to the skillet, solemn paces
At the stove, I cut the eggs another way
Promising

It makes a difference now
How I move my heart to you
I could get a half-moon haircut
Take two-step lessons
Scramble unto thee
Bring the bargains in

Dancing on my father's back comes to mind
Nestling a pine cone in the belly button of the Lord
Desperate, do anything

Raucous prayers among the rocks
Bacon, plans, remorse
People hide in little coastal towns
To savor them
But son,
You needed more than merriment
When you learned
Our Stella
En route to Rockaway
Crushed by a yellow school bus

Wretched
Riddle
I tried reaching you in Amsterdam

In delirium grew pine cones
Threw them in
Out came heaps of jeans your size.

Religion has a purpose.

Why I Like Bad Poetry

I still think it's livelier
than regular conversation,
an improvement over routine courtesies.

Moreover, it shows the devil is alive, well
and contemporary.

I like bad poetry because I like to write it
and my friends like to write it
and I like them.

Basically, I'm a friend of mistakes.
They warm my heart
like fat white pancakes
and Folgers.
It's safe to get out of bed knowing
another faultless day
of plain human error
expert self-deception
and helpless dishonesty
await me, knowing
my friends, too, will
enjoy their fair share.
All of it will help write our poetry.

Frankly, I'm afraid of inspired and perfect things,
Coming from God only knows where.

So I accept this elaboration of mistakes,
this straying off.
I'll be a drunk helicopter pilot with hiccups,
    With tears in my eyes, bouncing over the Cascades
    until the craft comes along—
    I know what I need:

A grand, a juicy mount with bronzed forehead,
a green stallion in trans-world flight.
Snorting flame, he'll slow down
then in a viridescent gust, brush me,
    Poet, love,
        come with me tonight!
        No more blubbering.
        Just hold on hard!

Section II

Hagar, Astyanax

Hagar: Genesis 16:1-16; 21: 9-21. I am also indebted to Phyllis Trible in her Texts of Terror for a discussion of Hagar. (Texts of Terror, Literary-Feminist Readings of Biblical Narratives, Fortress Press, 1984)

Hagar the Brave

Who dared to name the deity
The disappearing God
The One who abandons
The One who sees

She
Who believed the trickle
In the rock
Who lived the empty flask
Who said, in whose corner are you,
Sir,
Who upheld the I am not mine,
Who said
Go

Who lived to see water
Flow under fires,
Hagar
Descant now on our descent

The Return of Hagar

Sand-blistered Seer
Annotate your steps
From Beersheba
Unto our
Square
Make awake
We who maim

Bring water
You who lived the empty flask
The disappearing God
Loathing to convict, you
Named instead
The one who sees
Hagar, Muster
Sweetest intentions
Again investigate.

Night Madre, Be

My imaginary
Hammock of sonnets
Shadowing the helmets
Pickups with tusks

Be all this
My carnival
Receiver of unkempt sounds
Violent prayers revised

I've waited, exiled
Night Madre
Balm or miscarriage

Before Abraham was
You were thinking

Light of mine

Dark Madre, Be.

Beware the Laurel

Night Madre
Your brother, white stomach,

Under the laurel out back
We dare not tiptoe
Onto the porch, he's
Wheezing out scriptures
Knife dancing on the radish tops
Poised

Night Madre,
Is this your brother?
White stomach defying the sun
Unruffled, crushing towns, orchards
He who shelled the kindergarten,
From battlements, hurled theses

Night Madre
Return

Fondest madrigal
Return
To the killers among us

Dark water Illegal
Bind us again.

Night Madre Beholden

Way station unto
love
the
stunt divine

Give
surety
fitting for our chaos
madly advancing

nudge the
Jesuits peering
as if to know
as if at snow

Find the mom
with marmalade spilling
hoist her up the hill
to temple
shamrock covered
nurturant in each season

Be with her seasons Madre
Darling Girl
of God's old eye
steal us
unto worthiness.

Darling Night Madre

In your leisure look at our lack
In your gloomy luster behold our human
Imaginary

Speak, you must speak louder
Go with might

To our dark dead camps
Hear the children
Air sewn with grief

Now to bed
I will heed
Your
wounded coat.

Night Madre Forlorn

You befriended demons once
Now come back to us
Give and give again
Proverb, rhymed enigma
Truthed-up resonance
Fitting for our chaos

The deep is out of sync
Landed citizens upstream, gloating
Down, beg and trundling

Sweetest aspirations
go out hunting
but few cakes in larders
across the land.

Astyanax Did Not Die
for Elias

Heir apparent of Troy,
Son of Andromache and Hector,
Astyanax, by many accounts,
did not survive the city's sacking,
was hurled from the wall and died.
Others remember his small body
used to club old King Priam to death.

Let me tell you: Astyanax did not die.
Hidden by a phalanx of fierce children,
 he was hurried to a country where
sturdy old women
peel apples backwards
with plain paring knives,
peels landing in perfect spirals
on slabs of wood.

I say to you:
Astyanax founded a dynasty
kind and fair in
apportioning goods and plots,
where a council of old women
forbids the heaping up
of ordnance at the borders and store-housing of germs
where drones are merely the soothing hums of the council
and of apple spirals falling.

Astyanax, at Rest

Bedded in Lancaster hills
Infant dreaming
Wilderness
Seared wild peppers
Dandelions too intricate

Hecuba in emeralds, silent rubies
So distant she may neither see nor sense
Your stone enclosed refulgent pasture

You child
Startle us
Psyches unprepared
Your oblong thoughts
Wedged into our doldrums

Odysseus wishing you ill
Fashioned 30 pounds
Into club
To maim Old Priam
Failing this
His infantry foiling the design
Sprayed fire ants to your pasture

But. diligent baby
Unwilling to break old Hecuba's heart
From your clumpy home
Begged them to forego
Ill will and rancid spit

We wait ready for your entry
Our storm,
Story and furious flesh.

Astyanax, Please

Render your palms of thought when people
Starve themselves to death
Refusing also dirt and pebbles
Not merely ribs, elderberries, eggs

Heartbroken baby
Imaginary from the ancients,
Might you
Hurl divine spit
Across ages and galaxies
To our spot

You of gratitude
Who did not stop
Milking goats each dawn
Adopted a kid
Spurned by its doe

You, Little One,
Pitching buckets all over the Milky Way.
Enter our small sweat

Section III

Enigma, Neighbor

A Rusty Beard

Curls prickling outward,
The large African man at St. Andrew
Gold-plated cross on a chain
Pulled his dark, muscled neck downward—
A child snuggled into his right side

On his left, a visitor, rigid.
Reading her unknown face,
It appeared to ask
What happens here?
What can be guessed?
Might apostates
Have a place on the bench?
He glanced sideward, hummed

Here is the game room for broken hearts
Be seated
Here the queen of dark water holds sway

The visitor lowered her lids
When shall it begin?
What more then?
When shall it start?

My Neighbor

Nick lives on a speck of a street
that survived urban renewal.
An aging immigrant, he is ill, incontinent,
but still a gardener of note.

Nick wears filthy socks,
fondles a crucifix, then with crooked hands
hoists poles for beans and tomatoes,
drinking Chianti between rows
relieving himself where the cats do.
Nick, unknown to the mayor,
could feed a whole street, supply a school with
cucumbers and squash.
Last summer he gave me ears of corn
and called me honey,
said he needs a wife to clean his house.
Sitting on the steps alone,
his swollen hands hold a fresh fig,
and when he sucks the inside out,
I pretend that he is Neruda
about to explain a few things.

Enigma

If anything now
a tilt toward more disciplined sorrow
old prayers molting
mischiefs rated and arrayed.

The camellia early
and wondrous
the stats in Harper's facts
thrill on the skin
small relishments abounding.

But good people died
that's the difference
the terrible
difference.

Our engines and systems
inscrutably hygienic
forgetting the beat of
my kitty's heart and her purr.

A Kettle

Tonight I shined the kettle from Cairo
Bought with you at a hardware store
As we walked streets with shelves of flatbread
Nile oranges, bloods and sweets
Breakfast, flat beans and radishes
Man in a gray tunic serving

I bought the Cairo kettle to bring home
Since I could not bring you
Your genial patina, shadows
You who always sought
The stranger

You I learned were leaning into love
With someone I'd not yet met
Barely knew her, you said
She's Syrian, from Aleppo
In Cairo to study Arabic.

Tonight, ten years later
A gust of light whirls
In the courtyard
Of Berkeley family housing—
Daughter of you and the Syrian
No longer stranger but kin

I polish the kettle again
To the luster of you
Do not mind the dents it's borne

Have asked you to pack it in the walnut box
That will contain me
When I, dull, crepuscular
No longer thirst for tea
Or even you, heaven forbid.

Madison Street

For three days
an old woman
has been standing on her head
in a pile of ashes.

I have not called for help yet.
After all, she could be in love.
Or maybe she's the hag escaped from "Tartuffe."
She will go back when she thinks
the director has missed her.

Or she could have climbed out of a Playboy cartoon.
You know, one of those blue-hairs who beg
stagecoach drivers to rape them
right on the dirt trail.

Or what about Blanche DuBois?
Nobody really knows what happened
after matron took her off Stanley's
hands.

Those little feet sticking up—Grimm's Cinderella!
Old, with her own family problems now,
out for attention.

I don't know exactly what to do about
an old woman
upside down in a pile of ashes, and
I'm afraid to take action.
If this is a stunt by someone brilliant
I could wreck the show.
At least I could bring her a wedge
of ripe Bartlett pear.
They're in season and I have a bowl full.

Little Jasmine

Let's go find the rabbi laughing
Nausea had us fainting
Milk only made
The spinning worse
No red-spotted tongues
Shall follow us
Oh let us eat a berry tart

Run laughing with me
Little Jasmine
To the laughing rabbi
Eating key lime pie
and hot cross buns

Run then with the rummy poets
Little J
Sharper verdancies occur
Once solipsistic skies
Laugh down their bloated blues
Radiance will ensue

Let us
Listen to the rabbi laughing
We could visit meadows, J
Imagine dinosaur extinctions
Wandering comets
Lighting on our eyes

Let us be surprised
Unnerved exalted
Laughing rabbi
My little J.

True Selves

Today at the zoo I watched
a peacock unleash
its feathers,
the sight punishing me for waste

All this trouble, being human
and when my son said,
Mommy, I want to kiss the ostrich
I worried you, Love, would not
slide into my eyes again,
that they would turn to rocks

And what are we
decades later,
visiting the corner of the city
where the creatures are diminished,
small ourselves from old hurts
that stung and shrunk?

Or are we rising with
the great hawk in its cage?
No one,
not the homely tale teller from the core
nor that son with rainbows in his eyes
nor the man and woman bearing
holy water to each other

can explain the black elephants
of you and me.

What Must One Do To Be Saved?
Maryam Hazards the Question

Walk the white lab by the tulip tree
count the buds above while
the dog sniffs the trunk below.

Catch #12 to Central Library,
Look for a beleaguered soul warming himself.
Signal, through subtle eye movement,
a wrapped sandwich. Call the elected one out.
Should it be yourself, then quietly consume the gift.

Dust off the velvet hat and quickly discover
the black circus stallion.
With a partner in red leggings,
mount the beauty and fly off.

Locate Venice immediately.
Drag your party into the small boat
and behold the dark grey
lace clouds overhead.

Consider the fronds of Palm Sunday,
how they dry, designing themselves into crosses.
Press a red jewel from an old necklace
into the center point of a palm.
Dispatch it to a boy in Egypt.

Clothe yourself in the saffron sari you've been saving.
Wear the broken necklace (whose
jewel nests in the palm above).
Deck out to the utmost.
Hesitate not to wear sheer underskirts.

Invite the invalids with their mouths wide open
and ragged cries
into your cranium and willing bones.
Gown each patient in a sari,
remembering there is neither male nor female.
Hire the stallions to fly them away in their gauzy attire.

As you assemble the vessels, creatures, sites, peoples,
recall that those with full lips, bitten
concave cheeks, vagrant hearts,
are the delight of The Discovery,
and thus the project will continue.

Ballot Box

Trapped together in the ballot box,
we do not know if rescue is planned.
We do not know how this will end, if we will ever be allowed to return.
We are eating up the pencils.
We do not know if someone will slip in
some water, some bread.
We have been standing
so long our legs hurt.
We have heard reports where
neither sitting nor turning was allowed,
people stood in vomit and urine.
Here, no matter what positions we assume,
our faces are not far from each other.
We can muster some kind of friendship.
Unknown twists are not impossible in
this uncalled-for hot and tiny place.
Our mutual hunger, thirst, desire to do right
brought us here.
We decide to write in each others' names.